This bo

Hustle University (Hustle U) is an institution of higher learning for today's Independent Minded Entrepreneur.

The mission of **Hustle University** is to promote entrepreneurialism and leadership through personal development, empowerment and the teachings of proven success strategies.

www.HustleUniversity.Org

HUSTLE WHILE YOU WORK

Using Your 9 to 5 to Jump Start Your 5 to 9

HUSTLE WHILE YOU WORK

Using Your 9 to 5 to Jump Start Your 5 to 9

By Hotep

SKINNYMEN PRODUCTIONS

New York   Atlanta   Los Angeles

Hustle While You Work

www.hustlewhileyouwork.com

ISBN # 978-0-9800232-1-3

Published by: Skinnymen Productions, Stone Mountain, GA 30083

Skinnymen Productions, its logos and marks are trademarks of Skinnymen Productions.

Manufactured in the United States of America

Printed by Selfpublishing.com

First Printing, October 2007

Photography by OPP Studios

PUBLISHER'S NOTE: This work is a labor of love. It is the result of my attending the **School of Hard Knocks** where I received a B.A. in *Failed Ideas*, a Masters Degree in *Bad Investments*, and a PhD in *Poor Time Management*. Names, characters, places, and incidents are either the product of the author's experiences or are used with permission, and any resemblance to actual persons, living or dead, business establishments, events, or locales is entirely on purpose.

<u>DEDICATION</u>

I dedicate this book to everyone who leads the double life; working hard during the day, and even harder in the evening! This applies to entrepreneurs, students AND parents. GET YOUR HUSTLE ON!

ACKNOWLEDGEMENTS:

Redd- the only person that can sell my products better than me, **Ash-** (my baby brother) get money!, **Rasta-** the Fresh Maker, **Manny Blo-** Mancho Akh Baby! **Raheim Shabazz-** streets is watchin, **Al (Air Tran)-** thanks for the speedy check-ins, **Allen Johnston-** my mentor, **Ron Pramschufer-** a hustler from another mother, **Bro. Keidi-** liberation radio at its best, **Khaazra-** when RU moving to ATL?, **Dawnia-** you're an angel, **Mr. Brooks-** my financial guardian, **Queen-** the number one female hustler, **Randy Fling-** thanks for believing in my book, **Amir Shaw-** thank you for making me news worthy, **Universal-** your prediction was right; "it's my time to shine"!, **Rodney Lundy-** you need to write a book, **Velvet-** thanks for being in my corner, **Preiska, Jo & Tiffany-** true Black Stallions, **Vincent Alexandria-** you have wisdom beyond your years, **Shayna & Tara-** the revolution will be televised, **Lauren Yvette-** answer your phone!, **Dennis Byron-** thanks for putting me in the paper, **Angela Margerum-** you are beautiful!, **Lee May-** thanks for screening my movies in your theater, **Asa-** money doesn't matter, **Dante Marshall-** your support is much appreciated, Marvin **Arrington Jr.-** the hustlin' attorney, **- Yolanda Dryerbuzz-** keep it buzzin', **Veronica Hartwell-** I can always count on you, **Tyson Hall-** it's our turn!, **Rovella-** we're gonna have that meeting one day, **Rick Mcdevitt-** thanks for opening the door, **Momma Tonya-** that day changed my life, **Leticia & Avery-** for putting me on the cover of your 1st issue, **Mawuli Davis-** for being an advocate for young black males.

To all the contributing writers- thank you for reaching back to pull others forward. To those I thanked in the last volume and those I missed. I love you all!

TABLE OF CONTENTS

FOREWORD

HUSTLE WHILE YOU WORK (The Concept)

We live in uncertain times. Actually, life has ALWAYS been uncertain. From ancient times until today, there have been very few things that human beings could consistently count on forever. Ironically, the only thing that is *Constant* is **Change**.

Things are always changing. And likewise, we must also change to adapt to life's inconsistencies in order to **survive**.

Survival is the lowest level of existence. I assume that since you are reading this book, you don't want to just "survive", you want to **live**. Today, in order to live, we need MONEY; that is why we work.

Current events have shown us that our economy is unstable. Regardless of the industry, job, career, business or investment strategy, what goes up will eventually come down. Corporations go bankrupt, stocks fall, companies downsize, businesses close. No *one*......no-*thing* is immune to, or exempt from the laws of nature.

As savvy, independent-minded entrepreneurs, we must prepare for the different seasons of our business(es). This is why we **HUSTLE WHILE WE WORK**.

Who ever said you have to choose between working for an employer and working for ourselves?

Option 1: Work for an employer. Devote your time, energy and life to someone else's dream. Get paid consistently. Work longer hours in hopes of a promotion or bonus. If you lose your job in this scenario, you are in big trouble because your job is your **only** source of income.

Option 2: Work for yourself. Devote your time, energy and life to your own dream. Get paid inconsistently. If anything happens to you personally in this scenario, or your business hits an unexpected slump you are in big trouble because your business is your **only** source of income.

Why can't you do both? Work for an employer AND be self-employed. **Hustle while you Work!**

Option 3 (Hustle while you Work): Work for yourself AND work for an employer. Devote your time, energy and life to your own dream WHILE working at your job. Make a sometimes inconsistent income, BUT still get paid a steady paycheck. If anything happens to one income in this scenario, you can use the other to carry you through the rough time because you have **two** sources of income.

Get the picture?

The idea behind *Hustle while you Work* is nothing short of creating **Multiple Streams of Income** (MSI).

The concept of MSI basically expresses that we should create many opportunities for us to simultaneously generate income.

Don't put all your eggs in one basket.

Think of the farmer who plants various crops that bloom in different seasons. Different crops allow him to reap harvest from some crops during the summer and continue to profit from other crops during the winter.

The idea of **Hustle While You Work** recognizes the changing "seasons" in business. It allows us to reap *harvest* (profit) from some streams during the good times and continue to profit from other streams of income during the downturn.

You've probably heard Robert Allen or Robert Kiyosaki discuss the importance of creating *Multiple Streams of Income*. For the most part, they discuss this in reference to those that are solely entrepreneurs. The fact is though, NO MATTER WHAT YOU DO TO MAKE A LIVING, YOU ARE ALWAYS WORKING ON MULTIPLE TASKS. So the same concept of MSI can be applied **even if you work a 9 to 5**.

If you **Hustle while you Work**, you have at least 2 sources of income; one source of income that is consistent, yet limited; AND another one that may be inconsistent, but where the earning potential is LIMITLESS.

Never forget..... when we discuss your j-o-b, it is only as a temporary means of security, NOT as a lifetime sentence of servitude. This manual will help you see the benefits of, and give you the strategies to use your *job* to launch your **business**!

WHY THIS BOOK?

I've had the *idea* of this book for a few years. But it wasn't until the summer of 2007 that I decided to actually write it.

My main motivation for writing this book was *frustration*. I was tired of seeing the people around me being Broke, Busted and Disgusted (as my mother puts it).

Every one of these people had dreams of being successful entrepreneurs, but most were simply unable to turn their dream into a reality.

I've spent the last 11 years of my life trying to inspire and motivate people through teaching, counseling and creating edu-tainment products. My travels have led me to realize that this problem of wasted talent and unfulfilled dreams is widespread around the country.

People are looking for real, practical **answers**. They are tired of the old *Secret of Success* and *Get Rich Quick* scams that we find so common.

I've made it my personal practice not to focus on *problems*.........but to offer **solutions**. So, in keeping with this practice, I began to write this book to detail a success strategy that I call, *Hustle While You Work*.

Months later, I shared the idea with a friend of mine. He loved the idea so much, he wrote this to me:

Peace Hotep,

*I was once told, "**You can't be a light for the world if you can't pay your light bill**".*

The reason why so many people are unable to focus on succeeding is because they are too busy trying to SURVIVE. The cost of living is what many people are striving for, but are these people really living or just simply existing? As a result, these people go through life without contributing their voice, their creativity, or without making their mark in society. How do I know? I know because I used to be one of those people.

Since High School I had been in the rat race working various jobs to make ends meet. Over that time frame I gave two feeble attempts to pursue my entrepreneurial dreams, but was forced to put them "under the bed" for reasons of fear, lack of confidence and finances. I just couldn't leave my day job.

It took 20 years for me to realize 2 important things. One, I can be easily fired or laid-off (again). Two, I have a vision that has never been seen, a voice that has never been heard. It is time that I express that vision and that voice. I must get MY hustle on!

My education, various sacrifices, and job give me an advantage. I am a taxpayer in a position to contribute more than just daily labor to society. Since I can pay all of my bills, I can now focus on contributing my VISION!

I believe that all of us have visions that will improve our lives and those who are touched by our visions. Can you imagine going through this entire life just paying taxes, paying bills, reading the paper and watching various TV/Cable programs? If you spend too much time watching other people do things, then you will not spend enough time doing things for yourself. **Very few people get on TV by <u>watching</u> TV.**

Can you truly be happy without expressing your voice that can say things the world has never heard? I can not-- so I will not stop. I must **Hustle While I Work**. - Eugene E. Adams III

Needless to say, after reading this personal testimonial, I knew that if an intelligent, well-spoken college graduate could feel this way; the need for this book was even greater than I first thought. Writing HWYW became my top priority from then on.

-Hotep

WHY ME?

You might have heard of me before.

Some people know me as **Hotep**. Others know me as **Hustle Simmons**.

As owner of Skinnymen Productions, I've worn (and continue to wear) many hats. Depending on when and where someone has met me they know me as a: **CEO, promoter, rapper, music producer, artist, filmmaker, graphic designer, motivational speaker, filmmaker, director, author, vendor, publisher, writer, photographer, videographer, editor, event planner, consultant and publicist.**

Fans of my works know about my: **3 albums, 2 full-length documentaries, quarterly newspaper, audio CD, 2 books, 3 music videos, national tours, art exhibit, workshops, presentations, online video promotion clips, TV commercials, guerilla promotional tactics, out-the-box thinking and trendsetting product packaging.**

The Washington Post: February 8, 2007

What most people DON'T KNOW, is that I accomplished all of this over the past 10 years while being employed as **a full-time elementary school teacher**.

How am I able to accomplish this?

I *Hustle While I Work*.

*"I don't just write about it.....I **AM** ABOUT IT!"*

- Hotep

SETTING THE STAGE

A JOB VS. YOUR BUSINESS

"If money is the only reason for which you hustle, you have a job not a business."

Before we begin, it is important that we have a common understanding of certain terms and how they are used in this book.

Two words that will repeatedly appear are: *Job* and *Business*. Here are their definitions.

Job noun 1. a piece of work, esp. a specific task done as part of the routine of one's occupation or for an agreed price.
2. a post of employment; full-time or part-time position.
3. anything a person is expected or obliged to do.
4. an affair, matter, occurrence, or state of affairs.

Business noun 1. an occupation, profession, or trade.
3. a person, partnership, or corporation engaged in commerce, manufacturing, or a service; profit-seeking enterprise or concern.
6. that with which a person is principally and seriously concerned.
7. something with which a person is rightfully concerned.

I've written out these definitions for you to know the meanings of both of these words and the difference between the two. They **do not** mean the same thing.
Though they both have multiple definitions and uses the main difference is clear.

A **job** is referenced as a *temporary* state or a *single, minor* task to be performed in return for something of value. It is a *piece* to a whole and a *means* to an end.

A job is performed, completed and paid for.......the end.

A **business** however, is referred to as a more prominent state of affairs. It is the *whole* which requires multiple tasks (jobs) to operate. It is the major process that an individual is either *concerned with* or *engaged in*. The word **business** has a more defining quality. Almost as if it were a living being, a business is: born, named and nurtured so it can grow to become big and strong. Some businesses even "die".

My point in writing this chapter is to put things in proper perspective. There's nothing wrong with having a job with a boss. As noted earlier a job is a temporary situation, a means to an end. Your job is something you do; it **does not** define who you ARE.

There IS a problem though, when you have a **job**, but no BUSINESS.

Your hustle is your **business**; that which you are most concerned with. It is what you live for. It is why God put you on earth. It should consume your every thought because it is an integral part of your conscious being. (If your hustle is anything less, see BONUS CHAPTER entitled, "**Do You**".)

Your **hustle** is the one true business that you work for, even during the times when you work at a **job**.

Hustle While You Work.

- Hotep

HUSTLE (Defined):

While I'm at it, let me also expound on the word *hustle* and how it will be used in the context of this book.

1. Hustle- verb; to act aggressively especially in business dealings.

2. Hustle- noun; a side job. Work one does outside of their 9-5 job. (Similar to *moonlighting*)

The title: *Hustle While You Work* implies exactly what it says............ W-O-R-K! Hard work! There's no way around it folks.

In fact, *Hustle While You Work* means you are going to have to work TWICE as hard as your peers. First, you go to **work** at your job, then you get home and **hustle**, only to wake up early the next morning to go back to work! This lifestyle is not for the lazy or weak. It takes **strength, humility, commitment** and **diligence**.

If you possess these qualities (or are at least willing to learn), the information within this book will help you work SMARTER, instead of HARDER as you climb your personal pyramid of success and freedom.

For those of you that are admittedly lazy, weak (or both) please politely close this book and put it back where you got it.

NOTE:

Throughout this book you will see many references to the new entrepreneur's bible, *The Hustler's 10 Commandments*. If you haven't already, it is highly recommended that you read this book. In order to maximize your full potential you will need to understand these principles and how to apply them.

THE HUSTLER'S 10 COMMANDMENTS

1. YOUR NETWORK IS YOUR NET WORTH

2. IMAGE IS EVERYTHING

3. THE EARLY BIRD GETS THE WORM

4. IT'S LONELY AT THE TOP

5. SUCCESS- WHERE OPPORTUNITY MEETS PREPARATION

6. BUSINESS IS PERSONAL

7. EVERYTHING IS NEGOTIABLE, EVERYTHING

8. IT'S NOT *WHAT* YOU KNOW OR *WHO* YOU KNOW

9. IT TAKES DOUGH, TO MAKE BREAD

10. KNOW & BELIEVE IN THYSELF

CHAPTER 1

FROM SUPERMAN TO MAN:
DEALING WITH DUALITY

FROM SUPERMAN TO MAN

Your job is not an obstacle in the way of your entrepreneurial dream; your job IS THE WAY to your entrepreneurial dream. If you are a true hustler, you will learn to "flip" money and resources from your job and apply them to your business.

Think about it..........

We've discussed the similarity of Hustle While You Work to MSI. At the very least, whether you like your job or not, think about it simply as being one of your many streams of income.

With that being said, let's discuss the duality aspect an entrepreneur encounters when operating his/her own business and also working a 9-5.

When I started Skinnymen Productions in 1997, it was as a rapper/ Hip-Hop producer. After releasing 3 albums independently in Atlanta, GA, my marginal local success led to a decent amount of publicity. In 2001, it wasn't uncommon for the parents of the children I was teaching to say that they read about me in a magazine or saw me on T.V. This was very unsettling for me because at the time, I was making songs/ videos that were inappropriate for youth, and therefore, were in conflict with my image as a public school teacher.

For several years, I had been able to operate my music business silently; but as it grew, so did the need to create a split personality.

I call this need to create an alter ego, **"The Superhero Syndrome"**.

As an entrepreneur with a job, one might want to think of themselves as Superman. (I know Superman isn't as cool as Spiderman or Wolverine, but he is definitely the best hero to site for this example). Let me explain.

Superman is an extraterrestrial. He is SUPER human. In order to fit in with society he has to pretend to be Clark Kent: an average, tax-paying U.S. citizen. Why does he do it?

Why does the most powerful being on the planet work as a bumbling news reporter?

Because even a "man of steel" needs resources!

As Clark Kent the news reporter, Superman can make money to afford his worldly needs. He also uses his job as a way to stay informed about current events and activities so he can more effectively do his real work as Superman.

Superman hustles while he works! Saving the world is his *business*; collecting news as Clark Kent is just a *job* he performs to reach this goal.

YOU, (the independent-minded entrepreneur) are Superman. You are mighty and strong; faster than a speeding bullet. But at your job, you are disguised as Clark Kent….an underling, an employee.

This is the dual, split-personality complex that many entrepreneurs face today. There is no shame in it. It is A MEANS TO AN END. It is a way that thousands of entrepreneurs ensure the success of their business.

Remember, your 9-5 is temporary. It is a **job**. Your hustle is your **business**. *Up, up and away!*

TASKS:

1) Separate your job self from your business self.
2) Humble yourself at your workplace.
3) View your job simply as a *means* to an end.
4) Always remember that you are a great and mighty being.

While mostly fantasy, the dual life of Superman has a very real, human basis. Don't let your ego dismiss the value of its Clark Kent aspect. Both are equally necessary.

CHAPTER 2

KEEP YOUR DAY JOB: JOB BENEFITS

KEEP YOUR DAY JOB

Having a day job is a good thing, even for entrepreneurs. Besides the obvious financial benefit, there are many other ways you can profit from having a job. This chapter will discuss a few.

Medical/ Dental/ Life Insurance

The cost of insurance has been a major problem for small businesses since the 1980's. Insurance is expensive and continues to rise. Most large companies offer full-time employees insurance benefits. And it is usually much cheaper because of the group plan.

I (for one) am relieved knowing that I don't have to pay full price for medical/ dental services. **Man, they make a KILLING!** Even though I'm in good health and may only visit once a year, having the access and means to pay during those few, unexpected emergencies makes it well worth the low monthly payment.

The benefit of having insurance through your job multiplies when you have children and/or a spouse; especially *life insurance*.

Paid Vacations

There are few greater feelings than getting paid for laying on a beach, sipping a colada, doing ABSOLUTELY NOTHING! Having a full-time gig comes in handy during holidays and when you need a little relaxation, but don't want to worry if you can afford to take a break. Whether it's just 2 weeks or 2 months (like us teachers get), a paid vacation is a beautiful thing.

*Of course, if you **Hustle While You Work** you'll probably spend much of that vacation time on developing your business. But it still won't feel like **work**.*

Overtime

This is an area where you can really maximize your time and earnings at a job. I try to get as much overtime as possible. For many jobs, overtime simply means doing *less* strenuous work with *less* supervision for **more** pay. What a great concept!

Material Resources/ Equipment

This area is tricky, but I still had to list it. Depending on your job, you will have many resources available to you. Whether it's a computer, paper, copy/ fax machine, office supplies or postal services; access to these items is a major plus!

I say this area is tricky though because although you may have access to these things, it may not be appropriate (or legal) for you to use them for your own business. If you have a good relationship with your boss or supervisor however, it may not be a problem.

Imagine how much you'd save if you could simply use the equipment at your job as opposed to paying **Kinko's** or **Office Depot**. Their prices are ridiculous!

Networking

Companies, Organizations and Schools participate in industry conferences, seminars and training programs. These are great places to build your entrepreneurial network. I would recommend attending them whenever possible. It doesn't matter that the conference is unrelated to your entrepreneurial industry. As you network, you will find that some of the attendees will need the services that your business provides.

Even if you work at a high-traffic job like a grocery store, restaurant or gas station, there are opportunities for networking.

For example, it is rumored that **Denzel Washington** discovered **Derek Luke** while he worked his day job at a gift shop. Denzel gave Derek his first major role in the acclaimed movie, **Antwone Fisher**. After winning an award for this role, Derek revealed that 2 years earlier he was waiting tables. *Talk about lucky breaks!*

Ideas

One of my favorite perks of working at a job is the ideas I get from observing its daily operation and structure. Working a job (like having an internship), is an excellent real-life testing ground for your business.

At meetings, I peep the speaker's presentation style to see if/ how I can incorporate it to improve my own. I watch my boss's managerial techniques and also the employee's response to him to see what works and what doesn't work. At my job, I use their computer software not only to perform daily duties, but to see if I might want to use the same programs in my own business.

Treat your job like it was school, only at this institution you are getting **paid** to learn! If you view your job as an educational opportunity it will also make it more bearable to return to on a daily basis. Just like College, you go, learn, graduate and move on.

LIFE LESSON:

*My hustle is **Fishnett Ministries** which is a non-profit organization dedicated to youth ministry and development; during the day however, I use my MIT degree to work as a software engineer.*

*What I have learned at work is that corporate businesses really know how to complete projects **efficiently**, regardless of any obstacles.*

On the job, we used a computer program to track projects from beginning to end. It helps you organize tasks/ and better manage time. It predicts duration, projects costs and allows you to visualize all of this through a timeline. The program even helps you determine if any of the tasks are parallel or can be grouped together. It really assisted me in performing tasks in a much more synchronized and efficient manner. (My job was squeezing me for every second they could).

*Because I **Hustle While I Work**, I took those same task management concepts/ skills and used them in my own business. I used the exact same methods to produce **UnityFest** which is a quarterly urban gospel entertainment and networking event. During planning, I used my newfound knowledge to break the whole project into smaller tasks. Then, I used the concepts to distribute the tasks amongst my team to ensure that we complete the project in time. It worked like magic! I've held 3 profitable UnityFest events with even bigger ones on the way. Thank you job!*
– Biz Barrett

TASKS:

1) Enroll in your job's employee insurance plans.
2) Use your vacation time to advance your hustle.
3) Work as much overtime as possible.
4) Use resources/ equipment from your job only when appropriate or with permission.
5) Attend company sponsored conferences.

Everyone agreed that the morale and team-building session was a roaring success.

Contrary to popular belief, having a job can be advantageous even for entrepreneurs.

CHAPTER 3

TIME WAITS FOR NO ONE: TIME MANAGEMENT

TIME MANAGEMENT

Remember, you can always earn more money, but when time is spent, it is gone forever. **Zig Ziglar**

Of all the aspects of our lives, **time** is the most difficult part to manage. Unlike people or money, time is ALWAYS running out; and there's NOTHING we can do to slow it down or get it back.

Actually, the phrase *"time management"* sounds more like an oxymoron than a business term. How can one hope to manage something that is constantly AND consistently expiring? Nevertheless, in this chapter I will make a feeble attempt to do just that.

After my workshops, one of the most often asked questions is, *"Hotep, how do you find the time to do all of the things you do?"* I answer by saying, *"I don't find time...I MAKE time."* I never really understood the value of my response until I decided to write this book.

Consulting people has led me to realize that many individuals are *"busy doing nothing"*. They are active, but achieve very little because they are not concentrating on the right things. They focus on activity, but not on RESULTS.

The **Pareto Principle** or **"80:20 Rule"** argues that 80% of unfocused effort produces only 20% of the results and conversely, 80% of results are achieved with only 20% effort. I have personally found this to be a very valid equation in many people's lives, including my own.

Instead of "managing time", my focus has always been **how to make better use of time**. This focus has inadvertently led me to create a lifestyle in which I am able to maximize every second, minute, hour, day, week, month and year. Put simply, I achieved this habit by **categorizing**, **prioritizing** and **distributing** my activities.

Categorizing-

In my research, I've found that most people identify the following as the important categories in their life that they need time for:

1) **Work**
2) **Exercise**
3) **Eat**
4) **Sleep**
5) **Hobbies**
6) **Prayer**
7) **Family**
8) **Vacation/ Relaxation**
9) **Entertainment**
10) **Social**

The important categories in life that I make time for are:

1) **Personal**
2) **Family**
3) **Entrepreneurial**

See the difference?

If a person splits their time up ten different ways, then each aspect receives only **10%** of their time. But, (if they focused) they could condense many of these aspects into the "*Personal*" category, turn their hobby into an entrepreneurial endeavor and each can receive **33%** of their time. Imagine the possibilities!

Prioritizing-

My time is well spent because I also prioritize my tasks. For example, I listed my life's categories in the order of priority.

1) **Personal**
2) **Family**
3) **Entrepreneurial**

It is important that you *know* and *understand* this order of priority. There is a very dynamic relationship between these aspects of our lives. Your comprehension and ability to communicate this relationship to others will play a key role in your success in all three.

Personal life is first. You are number one! You are the *foundation* of the life that you *build*. If YOU aren't taken care of, there is no way you can take care of anyone or anything else. This third of your time is spent satisfying your need for food, clothing, shelter, health, and happiness.

Family is second because any one who is either married or has children (or both) knows that if home isn't taken care of, all other success is meaningless. This third of your time is spent satisfying the needs of others.

Entrepreneurial life is a close third. I say *close* because our entrepreneurial aspirations are often closely linked to our personal lives. In fact, much of our **personal** happiness is dependent on the state of our business.

For example:

Business is slow. I am not personally happy when my business is failing. Therefore, I feel the need to spend extra time on my entrepreneurial dream so it can be successful, so I can be happy. My wife however, is beginning to feel neglected because the extra time I'm spending on my business is coming from our family time that I would normally spend with her.

Another example:

My business is failing. It needs more of my time so it can be successful, so I can be personally happy. I need to take a few days off of work so I can get my business back in order. If I take off work, I won't get paid. Then, my family won't be happy because we may not have enough money to pay for our household needs.

Do either of these scenarios sound familiar?

Prioritizing helps you better deal with these common dilemmas by (1) knowing what's most important and (2) being able to better explain why you're having a dilemma in the first place.

"To Do" lists-

A person that hustles while they work feels like they have a million things to do. Don't try to rely on your memory for everything; **write down your daily tasks.**

Make a To-Do list.

To-Do lists not only help you remember the tasks you need to perform, they also help you see the progress that you are (or are NOT making).

Sometimes we feel overwhelmed with tasks; so overwhelmed that even when a day is over, we feel like we've accomplished nothing. A To-Do list will allow you to see exactly what tasks you have performed and give you a chance to appreciate your own hard work.

If, however, you are still dissatisfied with your progress, it's probably because your To-Do list is not **prioritized**.

People (myself included at times) make the mistake of doing things that are **urgent**, but not *important* before doing things that are *important*, but not **urgent**. When making to-do lists do so in order of priority so you can focus on the most important things.

Flow Charts-

A flow chart is a diagram that shows steps in a process or stages in a project. Much like an outline, flow charts are often used in business presentations to help the audience see a process or find mistakes in one. The Flowcharts help you analyze the number of steps and the time required for each step to more efficiently accomplish a determined goal.

By outlining a goal in a step-by-step flow chart you can concentrate better on each step because it will help you clarify your thoughts and have a more thorough understanding of the process. Thus, saving you a lot of time AND money.

Making time-

We often complain about not having enough time to do the things we want. And while I do agree that life is short, I also feel that most people can actually "make" more time if they simply changed their focus and some of their daily habits.

In my opinion, the average person is *lazy, greedy, shiftless, needy* and *unfocused*. They **sleep** too much, **eat** too much, **watch** too much T.V., **listen** to too much radio, **play** too many video games, **talk** too much, **chat** too much online, **drink** too much alcohol, **buy** too much junk, **smoke** too much, **dream** too much, **sex** too much and otherwise waste their life away.

In contrast, the independent-minded entrepreneur's daily activities consist of: **work, building, creating, nurturing, empowering, developing, learning, reading, researching, designing, negotiating, producing, directing, writing, teaching, exploring** and **investing**.

Take an honest look at your daily activities and decide whether or not they are in line with your own **personal**, **family** or **entrepreneurial** goals. Replace those that are not in line with some that are. Once done, you'll see that you've miraculously "made" more time for you to Hustle While You Work.

LIFE LESSON:

I have a family of three: My Wife, My Son and Myself. I have a day job as a Top Leasing Consultant in Atlanta, Ga. I own and operate a successful Marketing Company. (Redd Marketing). I work this hard because I know it takes Dough to Make Bread (Hustler's Commandment # 9) and I have set goals in my life that I want to accomplish.

At times working so hard can be very difficult for my Family and I. My wife requires and deserves attention, as does my 10-year-old son. I balance my entrepreneurial life by incorporating my family as much as possible. Example: If I can take my family out with me to a business function, I will. This gives my family first hand insight into what I do as a Business Owner and what is required of me when I'm out on business.

Communication is the glue that keeps everything together. Calling home, leaving notes, and checking in is a must. By staying in touch with my family/and business clients it allows little room for errors and misunderstanding.

*I use a planner (organizer) and keep it updated. I post a calendar inside my home and **keep it updated**. By keeping an up-to-date Calendar posted inside my home it allows my family to know my schedule, which keeps everyone on the same page.*

I also separate my "Me Time" from my business and home time. I try to allow 30 minutes to an hour a day with no interruptions for my family.

By Communicating, Planning, and setting aside Personal "Me-Time", you will find that separating your personal, family, and entrepreneurial time is not too hard to balance. -Nicholas "Redd" Scott

TASKS:

1) **Make a To-Do list.**
2) **Categorize and Prioritize your activities.**
3) **Do IMPORTANT tasks before doing *urgent* tasks.**
4) **Utilize flow-charts.**
5) **Stop *wasting* time and start MAKING time.**

CHAPTER 4

MAKE MONEY WORK FOR YOU:
FINANCING YOUR HUSTLE

FINANCING YOUR HUSTLE

In The Hustler's 10 Commandments, we established that it takes **dough** to make *"bread"*. This is probably the main reason why any of us hustle while we work. Of course, there are many ways to finance your entrepreneurial endeavors. Besides working, other common options include:

- investors
- sponsors/ advertisers
- inheritance
- prizes
- loans
- stealing

Each of these options has its own set of pros and cons. None of them will be discussed in this book. These methods of finance (for the most part) require you to place your dream on hold until someone else gives you money. Hustlers don't wait for opportunity, they create it.

This chapter will only detail methods that will help YOU MAKE MONEY, and then help your MONEY MAKE MONEY. The whole idea is to work, invest in yourself and pay yourself back (with interest).

Disclaimer:

I am not an expert on finances, but I've come to develop a wealthy lifestyle by applying knowledge that I've acquired from personal trial and error,
self-made millionaires, financial advisors, CPA's, CEO's, and specialists.

As a working, tax-paying American citizen, I take full advantage of the legal capitalistic opportunities, options and tax breaks that this country makes available to its citizens. In this chapter I will discuss a few of them, but I must make clear that *I am not attempting to give any financial advice.*

The following text in this chapter is to be used for information only, not as advice. Please consult a certified accountant and/or a financial planner before implementing and executing any of the strategies discussed in the areas of finance and taxes.

OK? Then let's begin.

People say that our capitalist society is designed for "the rich to get richer and the poor to get poorer". In many ways this is a true statement. However, it doesn't have to be. **Access to information** is the key to the door of financial independence and wealth. At one time, many practices were only accessible by upper class families. They kept the information amongst themselves and passed it down from generation to generation. Though this practice continues, today's technology-information boom has leveled the playing field.

The truth is, the same money management techniques used by the wealthy are available to everyone (yes, even YOU). The reason people do well is because they know and apply basic rules of **how money works**.

The average person spends the majority of their adult life working for money. Wealthy people however have learned how to make money, **work for them**. This is a key mentality for those who hustle while they work. We must actively and consistently find ways to make our money work for us.

Inflation:

I want to start by discussing inflation because I think this will put everything else into perspective.

Inflation is the increase in prices, or the decrease in the purchasing power of money. Remember when comic books used to be 60 cents? Now they cost well over a dollar. Comics haven't changed that much, but the value of $1 has changed a lot.

Last I checked, the inflation rate was about 4%. Is your savings plan taking this into account? I speak to many people whose savings plan consists of money in a bank account that accrues NO INTEREST. Others keep their savings in a personal safe or "*under the mattress*". I have heard a few proudly say that they have a Money Market savings account at a bank. But all too often even this kind of savings is not enough.

Let's say the inflation rate is **4%**. And your fixed interest bearing Money Market "savings" account gives you a rate of **3%**. At this rate, after adjusting your account's value by the rate of inflation, **you are actually losing money every year!** Thus the saying, "Poor people *save*, wealthy people *invest*."

401(k) Savings:

Since you are working (or need to be), let's discuss the 401(k). A 401(k) plan is an employer-sponsored retirement plan that allows a worker to save for retirement while deferring income taxes on the saved money and earnings until withdrawal. Many companies' 401(k) plans also offer the option to purchase the company's stock. If you're lucky, your employer will match a portion of your contribution. Your employer wants you to participate in the plan because of compliance issues. The matched amount they offer (the free money part) is your incentive to participate.

401(k) contributions are made on a pre-tax basis, which can greatly reduce your tax bill. Generally, if you contribute $100 a month, you've reduced your income taxes by $25 (assuming you are in the 25% tax bracket). So, your $100 contribution costs you only $75. The tax savings are magnified as your contribution increases.

IRAs:

Many people think that tax shelters are only for the wealthy. Yet thousands of people fail to take advantage of a tax shelter that's right under their noses!

An Individual Retirement Account (IRA) is a brokerage account that allows earnings to compound over time on either a federally tax-free or tax-deferred basis.
An IRA is probably the most popular and advantageous retirement savings vehicle available after a 401(k).

IRAs are a good way to save money for retirement because of their tax-favored status. By starting an IRA, you can defer (hold-off) paying taxes on your IRA earnings. Since these earnings grow without being taxed, more money will compound and work harder for you than if income taxes were taken out each year. When ready to withdraw, you're only taxed on the earnings gained, NOT the principle amount you put in.

With a Roth IRA, you have another way to save on taxes. Contributions to a Roth IRA and their earnings are allowed to grow tax deferred and be withdrawn tax-free as long as the Roth IRA account has been open at least five years and you are at least age 59 1/2 when you begin withdrawing the proceeds. No taxes paid on contributions OR earnings.

Bank Savings:

Banks are great! I have a few bank accounts. But a bank account is just one aspect of a wealthy person's financial picture.

Ever wonder how banks make so much money? Well, besides charging monthly fees and other small annoying charges, they make money by investing **YOUR MONEY!**

Ever wonder why many bank accounts have "minimum" balance requirements? Ever wonder why you get penalized for withdrawing money before a certain period of time? The more money you let them "hold", the more money they make by playing the market (with **YOUR MONEY**)!

That is why you are "awarded" for being a long-time account holder or for keeping large sums of money in your account. They pull very high interest profits. Even with the fluctuations of today's market, financial institutions can offer to pay you a small, "guaranteed" interest on your money market account because your "guaranteed" interest is just a small portion of the profit they already made (with **YOUR MONEY**)!

Why not learn to invest for yourself?

Investing:

Investing is just like gambling; sometimes you win, sometimes you lose. You **do not** have to be rich to invest. My financial advisor taught me that there are only 2 things you need in this country to make money:

Time and **Money.** Since you are already using your *time* to hustle while you work, let's invest some of that *money* so it can go to work too!

Investing is best viewed as a long-term activity. History shows that the longer you invest, the greater your potential for gain. It's time in the market that makes the difference. Experts say market "timing" is a bad way to invest because no one knows how the market will perform.

Matching your level of risk to your age and circumstances is a popular way of investing. If you're young, you can afford be more aggressive. If approaching retirement, a conservative fund might be better. Most people I know have a diversified (balanced) portfolio. This means that they invest in both aggressive AND conservative funds of varying degrees.

Historically, the market has always rebounded after periods of decline. Through systematic investing and a concept called *dollar-cost averaging*, you can take advantage of market fluctuation and buy more shares. **Dollar-cost averaging** means investing a certain fixed amount each month regardless of what's happening in the stock market.

Here's how it works:

When the market falls and your share price goes down, your monthly investment can buy more shares than when the market is up and your share price is higher. Over time, as the market rises again, those "extra" shares bought in a down market can increase the value of your portfolio.

Instant money:

So you think you don't have any money to invest. WANNA BET? I'm sure you can literally "find" money, laying around you right now.

Here's an example:

Suppose you buy two cans of soda from a vending machine at work each day — That's:

.75 per soda
X 2 sodas per day
= $1.50
X 20 work days a month
= $30/ month spent on sodas!

That's $30 spent on sodas ALONE! **Imagine** if you had a spouse! **Imagine** if I used a $3 cup of coffee in this equation instead of soda. That's **$120** per month!

Kick your soda/coffee habit and drink water instead (it's free and healthy!). Just by making one small change in your daily activities, you have made "instant money"!! There are probably many more situations like this in your daily life that could be used to free money for investing. Think about it: chips, snacks, candy, cigarettes…etc. Most of these daily habits you could do without anyway!

Automatic Deductions:

Saving/ investing money effectively requires consistency. I will be the first one to admit that I don't have the discipline it requires to withhold the same amount of my hard earned money on a consistent basis, only to deposit it into an account that I'm not supposed to touch. *DO YOU?*

If so, GREAT! But if you're like me and millions of other human beings it's hard to be so dogmatic. That's why I love automatic deductions.

Automatic deductions take the imperfect *human* factor out of the equation. Let a computer take money directly from your check or bank account every month and deposit it for you (known as direct deposit). You can sign up for it either through your bank or through your employer and designate **when**, **how much** and **where** the money will go. I think it's best to have your money deducted from your check through your employer (just like taxes). That way you don't even get a chance to see it. At first it might sting a bit not to have the additional money in your pocket. But soon enough, you would forget that you even had this "extra money". Chances are, you would naturally adjust your lifestyle and spending habits to fit the crunch. So you would be forced to **spend less** or **make more**; either way, you've just found another way to place yourself in a better financial situation.

Taxes:

The number one pimp in the world, **Uncle Sam,** won't let you live (or die) without paying him. As an employee, you pay taxes. As an entrepreneur (or self-employed individual) you are also responsible for paying taxes. In general, Uncle Sam wants a cut of every dollar you make. Wealthy people know how NOT to get pimped.

I'm not even going to **try** to discuss tax law. That's why I have a good CPA. He keeps me up-to-date with the latest changes in tax law so I don't pay any more in taxes than I have to. Of course the best place to get answers about taxes would be from the **Internal Revenue Service**.

68

TASKS:

1) Get a financial advisor.
2) Save AND invest your money.
3) Think beyond your local bank.
4) Explore IRAs.
5) Utilize automatic deductions.
6) Find ways to minimize your taxable income.
7) Pay your taxes.

Sixty people.
Total annual income is $3 million (and 65 cents).
Average annual wage is therefore $50,000.
Yep, the economy is going just GREAT!

CHAPTER 5

CUTTING COSTS: THE BEST THINGS IN LIFE ARE FREE

THE BEST THINGS IN LIFE ARE FREE

Savvy businesspeople (especially those that hustle while they work) find creative ways to cut expenses. The best way I know how to cut expenses is to get things for FREE. Some ways we hustler's get free stuff is through *partnerships, bartering* and by having *interns.*

Strategic Partnerships

Hustler's Commandment #1: *Your network is your net worth.*

As an independent-minded entrepreneur you will likely wear many hats. In many small businesses the CEO, director of marketing, secretary, publicist and web designer is often the same person. This occurs not because people enjoy doing so many different things, but because they can't afford to pay someone else to do it for them. If you find yourself becoming a Jack of all Trades, but master of none; you can find relief in strategic partnerships.

A common mistake new businesses make is trying to "hire" others to do work for them. This method requires one party to pay another for its products or services. Instead of hiring, you might consider partnering with other businesses.

Everybody needs help. And just like you need other businesses services, other businesses need yours. In a strategic partnership you use your area of expertise and combine it with someone else's creating a stronger and more time efficient business model.

LIFE LESSON:

*I started ERAJ Media with the knowledge I gained from undergrad and the love for cinematography. One of the first problems I ran into was trying to find clients. I had no sample reel or footage of my work to prove to a potential client that I could do the job. There was nothing separating me from Joe Blow on the street with a camera. I didn't even have my **own** camera at the time.*

One day I ran into a CEO of a budding film company who also had needs. He needed a production team to film his debut documentary and I needed footage for my reel. JACKPOT!!! The partnership worked perfectly! His company got a professional staff to film his documentary and my company got tons of footage and free video equipment rental.

The documentary we made was a national success; this built brand awareness and marked ERAJ Media as a production/post-production powerhouse. From the money my company saved, I was eventually able to invest in my own equipment that allowed me to grow the business and apply for even larger contracts.

Today, my company is doing very well. My business includes large weddings, annual corporate parties and consistent post-production work. ERAJ Media has just secured a 3-year contract with Morehouse School of Medicine and we completed the post production for comedian/ actor Nard Holston's Standup DVD, Nard's World.

If it weren't for that partnership I would have still been on first base right now. The moral of the story is that you can't do everything. If everyone does a little, no one has to do a lot. - Wesley Walters

Bartering

Bartering services is the KEY for small businesses. Bartering is simply exchanging services/ goods of equal value. Why should two capital poor companies spend money, when they can trade?

The main difference between bartering and partnering is that bartering goods/ services does not require your business to becoming publicly associated with another. Simple bartering is like casually dating someone without giving titles to the relationship or letting other people know about its existence.

Sponsors

The only type of OPM (other people's money) that I accept is from sponsors. Sponsors/ advertisers are basically people or companies who believe in you, or what you do, to the extent that they will PAY YOU to keep doing it so they can attach their name to it. If your business is doing GOOD things and becoming well known, look for companies that might want to advertise on your promotional materials, advertisements or at your events. You give them space on your flyer, ad or commercial and charge THEM to cover the cost!

For example: Your company has a reputation for distributing flyers throughout a given city. You create a new flyer. It costs $300 to get 5000 flyers. You charge a company $400 to place their logo on the back of your flyer. POW! Your cost is covered AND you pocket $100!

Another way is to go in half with a non-competitive company. They get one side; you get the other side of the flyer.

The same principle works on commercials, radio ads, concerts/shows, print ads…etc.

Interns

Another way to cut down on expenses is to "hire" *interns* instead of employees. An intern is someone who works for a company in return for experience in a particular field or for class credits. Depending on the arrangement, some interns are paid for their work.

High Schools, Colleges and Universities are filled with young, energetic students just waiting for some real-world experience. Many of them will JUMP at the opportunity to work for, assist, or just be associated with a budding business that is on the rise.

The best part is that interns are often motivated to do a really good job because your success makes them look equally as good. A wise intern will also use the opportunity to work for you to build their own network and resume. *You see, interns hustle while they work too!*

TASKS:

1) **Create strategic partnerships.**
2) **Barter services.**
3) **Seek sponsors for your events and promotional material.**
4) **Use interns whenever possible.**

CHAPTER 6

MANAGE YOUR BOSS

MANAGE YOUR BOSS

Entrepreneurs are a special breed of person. They are natural leaders and often very stubborn. *Independent minded people* are free thinkers; and do not follow directions well. They question authority and walk to the beat of their own drum. Therefore, an **independent-minded entrepreneur (YOU),** in the workplace is twice the headache for a "boss".

In this chapter we will briefly place ourselves in the boss's shoes so we can better understand his position, sympathize with his feelings, predict his behavior, communicate and therefore, more effectively hustle while we work.

A boss is an overseer. His/her role is to manage, regulate and lead. Besides hiring and firing employees, the boss is responsible for accounting, legal matters, budgeting, insurance and bills. A boss's job can be rewarding, but it is often very stressful because when things go wrong, he/she is held accountable. The position of a boss is a lonely one indeed.

Just like on any plantation in the 1600's, the boss only wants his/her workers to do what they're told, when and how they're told to do it. This enables the overseer to maintain order. The absolute LAST thing a boss wants is a "**free**" thinking worker on his plantation.

The independent-minded entrepreneur is dangerous to the operation of modern day plantations (*the work place*). Their natural leadership conflicts with that of the boss. Their "free" thinking ways are contagious; and if spread to the other workers can cause widespread chaos and mass exodus. Put short, **the independent-minded entrepreneur poses a direct threat to the authority and control of the Boss.**

There are basically 2 types of bosses:

1) The *Manager*-boss
2) The *Owner*-Boss

The *Manager*-Boss:

If your boss is the manager he/she is in a very delicate position. This boss has to maintain control of employees, run the operation AND constantly prove his/her own worth to the **owner** of the company. Because of this pressure from both sides, the manager-boss is doubly threatened by the presence of an independent-minded entrepreneur (YOU).

The **manager-boss** is threatened by you because:

- Your independent "free" thought may spread to your drone-like coworkers.

- Your leadership ability might be desired by the owner, and therefore weaken your boss's own job security.

Human and animal psychology teaches that if someone feels threatened, they in turn become antagonistic to the perceived threat. Likewise, because he/she feels threatened, the manager-boss is likely to treat you unkindly. **This type of boss will see you beginning to fly, and will attempt to clip your wings.**

To avoid this unpleasant experience and tension in the workplace, unless you have a great personal relationship with the manager-boss, you should keep your entrepreneurial endeavors and free thought a secret.

If this boss **is** aware of your goals, it is extremely important that they are assured that you DO NOT want their job and you are not going to cause any "trouble".

The Owner-Boss:

If your boss is the owner, the relationship is often very different. This boss is secure in his/her position. While your "free" thought is still contagious to co-workers, in the owner's eyes, this characteristic along with your leadership potential make you a perfect candidate to become a **manager**.

This is a trap for the independent-minded entrepreneur! While it is an honor to be offered the promotion, unless you desperately need the money you should politely DECLINE.

Owners are always looking for competent people to run (oversee) their company. If you fall into the trap and take the position, you also take on the added stress, responsibility and longer work hours. You become the **manager-boss**!

This is not what you want. You are the independent-minded entrepreneur. You are hustling while you work. Your goal is to use your job as a temporary means to help you build your business. You want the highest paying job, with the most freedom, requiring the least amount of responsibility and time commitment. Don't let the owner trap you into becoming the overseer of his plantation.

If your entrepreneurial goal is non-competitive with his/hers, try telling the owner about your endeavors. In this scenario, the probability is low that he/she will fire you because you have already proven yourself to be a valuable member of the team. He/ she is likely to be supportive of an entrepreneurs dreams. The owner of the company you work for could become a great mentor or potential partner for your own!

It is vital that you understand these variables in relation to your boss. Although he/she may be threatened by you, **YOUR BOSS IS NOT YOUR ENEMY.** There's no need for you to turn your work environment into a *war zone*. In the workplace, you must take the pathway of least resistance.

Since you now understand the role and responsibilities of a boss, you can effectively manage one! Humble yourself. Do what your boss asks you to do cheerfully, without question. Though your boss may initially seem defensive, if you treat him/her in a respectful and cooperative manner, he/she will normally do the same.

The bottom line is……you want your job to be as easygoing and enjoyable as possible, so you can continue to hustle while you work.

LIFE LESSON:

Shoot! I have two full time jobs; one as a mother, another as a corporate executive. I work at Coca-Cola and my boss is very cool. I was kinda worried in the beginning though. I didn't want to tell anyone at my job that I was an actress. When I started taking acting classes, I had to tell my boss that I was in school so I wouldn't get asked to work over time. I didn't want my boss (or co-workers for that matter) to know about my hustle because I kind of felt like they would start judging me in some ways. So I kept it to myself for awhile.

I eventually broke the silence when I started to do plays. While I was doing theater, the only way we got paid was to sell tickets. So I had to ask people at work, including my boss, to buy tickets. Man O' Man did they come out to support me!!! They even asked me for autographs. My boss was totally excited for me. She began telling guests that I was the "resident actress"; and even put me in a few Coca-Cola commercials.

I always meet my job's needs so I don't have a problem when it comes to making requests for my own business needs. For the most part, I use my vacation time and personal allotted time to take care of my business so I don't have to tell my boss too much. If I need to, I also purchase extra vacation days so that I can do what I need to do and not hurt my job performance.

*My boss is pretty flexible, but I would never ever want to be in her position. You see, I'm already a boss! I help other people in entertainment industry. That's **MY HUSTLE**. I started off as an actress. Today I am also a filmmaker, fashion show producer and CEO of my own production company. I always tell people "YOU are in charge of YOUR destiny, so don't give up on YOU!!"* -Yolanda Zellous

TASKS:

1) **Be careful with whom you share your business endeavors.**
2) **Be kind, respectful and pleasant to your boss.**
3) **Remember: Your boss is NOT your enemy.**
4) **Don't get trapped by a promotion that requires too much of your time and responsibility.**

When Mr Despo boasted that he had a clear, "no crap" management style, no-one argued.

*Be careful with whom you share your entrepreneurial aspirations. Remember the idea is to **use** your job, not LOSE your job.*

CHAPTER 7

THE FORK IN THE ROAD: TAKING THE LEAP OF FAITH

TAKING THE LEAP OF FAITH

Eventually (and hopefully) if you hustle *long* enough, *hard* enough and *smart* enough, you will reach a point where your **hustle** and your **work** start to conflict with each other. You will notice that, in order for your business to continue to grow, you need to invest more time and energy into it. This is when you begin to ask yourself that one, life-changing question:

Is it time for me to quit my job and pursue my entrepreneurial dream full-time?

How will you know when the time is right for you to quit your job? We've all heard the success stories of people who have quit their horrible day job and now make tons of money running their own business. We get sold these stories every day through infomercials, magazine ads web spam and radio spots. Network marketing companies are notorious for their use of these rare success stories to validate themselves.

But what you DON'T see is the millions of people, who lost their savings, homes and spouses because they left their day jobs too soon.

Let me be clear by stating that I am in NO WAY trying to scare people into not taking the great *leap of faith* to pursue their dreams. I AM however, attempting to help people make better, wiser, more informed decisions so that their "leap of faith" doesn't become a suicidal plunge to their death!

On the following page are some things to consider before leaving your job to pursue your business endeavors full-time.

1) Income Consistency- Are you able to make the minimum amount needed to run your business month after month?

2) Legal Liability- Have you taken into account the legal liabilities that you will be held responsible for as a business owner and the cost of insurance?

3) Insurance- Will you be able to afford the cost of Medical, Dental and Life Insurance for yourself, your family or employees?

4) Cost of Doing Business- How are you going to pay for your daily/ monthly business expenses?

5) Profit Margin- Will you be able to make enough profits from your business to save and invest?

6) Lifestyle- Will you be able to maintain you/ your family's current lifestyle? If not, will you be able to adjust?

If, after considering all of these factors, you decide that the time is right…..then **GO FOR IT!**

Me? I have personally opted NOT to leave my day job.

Although business has grown astronomically for me over the past five years, so has my lifestyle, and therefore, my **expenses**. The major events that have impacted this most were: *1) getting married, 2) buying a new home 3) going back to school.*

These events have upgraded my lifestyle to a point where I have much more financial responsibility than I had when I was single and lived in an apartment with a roommate. In order to maintain my current way of life (including health benefits, insurance, 401-K savings and wifey's shopping) my hustle needs to **consistently** bring in TWICE the amount I make as a teacher. I haven't reached that point yet.

I can't brag that Skinnymen Productions is my sole means of income. I do have a day job. **SO WHAT!?**

I love my job. I love my wife. I love my home. I love my life.

I travel the country. I make profits. I live in a large house. I have fun. I impact the world in a positive way. I turn my creative ideas into tangible products. I have savings and investments. I am a boss. I live life on my terms. I have options. I am free.

Success is measured by quality of life, NOT quantity of money. - Hotep

TASKS:

1) **Be cautious when considering leaving your job.**
2) **Always exit your job on the best of terms with your employer.**
3) **DO THE MATH!**
4) **Consider your whole life's picture, not just your immediate financial needs.**

Note

If you've reached the point where your business begins to consistently conflict with your work, but still doesn't generate enough money for you to quit, you may want to consider hiring an assistant or other type of part-time employee. A good assistant will free up your time as well as help shoulder the increasing growth of your business.

CHAPTER 8

MAKE MONEY WHILE YOU SLEEP: CREATING MSI

MAKE MONEY WHILE YOU SLEEP

The ultimate goal of *Hustling While You Work* is to achieve financial freedom through entrepreneurship.

As you arrive closer the point where you can comfortably "fire your boss", you may find a stronger need to continue the strategy of creating **Multiple Streams of Income** (MSI). For this chapter I've solicited the help of money-making experts for advice.

According to Michele Pariza Wacek of Creative Concepts and Copywriting LLC, 2 major reasons for creating Multiple Streams of Income are:

1. Make money while you sleep.
2. Leverage your time.

Basically, she's saying that you need to create streams of **Passive Income.**

PASSIVE INCOME:

Passive Income is one where money is received usually on a regular basis, without continuing effort.

(Note the key phrase….. "*continuing effort*". Passive Income does not mean requiring NO EFFORT at all; most passive income streams require great effort to start with.)

Making money while you sleep.

As mentioned earlier, the biggest problem for entrepreneurs (especially service providers) is **TIME**. Most small business owners ARE their business. The business is totally dependent on their personal performance. These entrepreneurs spend the bulk of their time making (or trying to make) money. BUT, when they aren't working, **they aren't making money**. That means, every time they sleep, rest or perform any other non-business activity, they are literally LOSING MONEY. Imagine going on a "2 week" vacation!

Michele Wacek suggests that entrepreneurs (especially service providers) **create a product(s)** to sell in addition to their services. This would create passive streams of income and help you better maximize your time (yes, even when you sleep).

Leverage your time.

With passive streams of income, you can more efficiently use your time doing something else while still making money. That "something else" can also generate income for you, so you're making money from two avenues of income (Multiple Steams).

According to Wacek, the trick to making multiple streams of income is to work on one stream at a time, until each can operate off of its own momentum.

So, if you start a venture, get it to the point where it starts to generate income. Once there, let it work for you **passively** while you work on the next project. You've just leveraged your time to maximize your earning potential!

MSI ONLINE:

According to Melanie Schwear in her article, *"How to Create Multiple Streams of Income Now"*, here are some ways to create multiple streams of income online:

Google Adsense or Other PPC Networks

If you have a good flow of traffic to your website, you can create a stream of income from Google Adsense. Just put their link on your site and get paid a percentage of advertisement money if a visitor to your site clicks a link in the ad box.

Affiliate Marketing

Make commission by selling another company's products or services. Get paid if visitors sign up for, or purchase, something after they click the affiliate link on your site.

Text Link or Banner Advertising

If you have an active site with a good amount of daily visitors, you will have little problem selling text link or banner advertising space on your front page. The more traffic your website has, the more people will pay to get on it. Sell monthly, yearly, or permanent links.

Drop Shipped or Wholesale Products

Sell tangible goods or information products such as ebooks and reports in this way. You can create multiple streams of income by offering multiple product lines.

Create a Subscription Section

Offer a member's only section on your website. With a low monthly subscription fee, people will pay to access secret information, pictures, music, an exclusive community, or anything you else can think of!

LIFE LESSON:

While myspace has been a great way to promote for many and make money for some, it's not really "YOUR" or "MY" space. I've always advocated that people register their own domain name and create their own website or blog space.

Besides selling an mp3 download, audio book, ebook, special report, video or podcast, you could give away information to entice visitors to frequent your site. By giving something away for free, your site or blogs traffic could increase significantly over time, making it ideal for companies and other individuals to advertise, ultimately adding another way for you to make money online.

I use this method with blogs I maintain. Essentially, I give valuable information, resources and links to help people make money online. As I continue to update the blogs and websites with valuable information, resources and links they continue to return. More than likely they'll create a link from their site to mine increasing the traffic to my blog even more. As more people frequent the Blog it becomes a great place for advertisers to place their ads.

Some of my sites that make me the most money are the ones that have a wealth of content and inbound and outbound links. Inbound links from highly qualified sites and blogs will greatly increase my search engine ranking. I acquire links from sites and blogs that are related to mine that rank high in search engines and themselves have a significant number of inbound links and a wealth of content. By getting a significant number of highly qualified inbound links to my websites and blogs, I dramatically improve the chances of my sites listing high with search engines and directories, thereby boosting my unique visitors or traffic. For an example of how you could make money online with a blog or website with targeted content, sponsored links and advertisements visit moneygoldmine.blogspot.com – Jawar

THE FINAL ANALYSIS

The bottom line is: Success requires work. Not only **hard** work, but *smart* work.

Of course, not all jobs are the same and there are many variables that we each need to take into account. But after reading **Hustle While You Work**, at the very least your mind is now open to the limitless possibilities and opportunities that your 9 to 5 offers you.

Your day job is not an obstacle. Your boss is not your enemy. The only thing that can come between you and entrepreneurial success is...... YOU!

TOP JOBS TO GET YOUR HUSTLE ON:

1) **Teacher**
2) **Substitute Teacher**
3) **Bartender**
4) **Waitress**
5) **Coach**
6) **Writer for Magazine/ Newspaper**
7) **Police Officer**
8) **Radio/ TV host**
9) **Married to a Celebrity**
10) **Intern**
11) **College Professor**

BONUS CHAPTER

DO YOU:
FINDING <u>YOUR</u> COMMODITY

Value No One Can Steal

"If you create and market a product or service through a business that is in alignment with your personality, capitalizes on your history, incorporates your experiences, harnesses your talents, optimizes your strengths, complements your weaknesses, honors your life's purpose, and moves you towards the conquest of your own fears, there is ABSOLUTELY NO WAY that anyone in this or any other universe can offer the same value that you do!" **- Author unknown**

DO YOU!

Starting and maintaining a business takes a lot of work, time, money, motivation, planning, research and talent. A failed entrepreneurial dream is often more due to one's own poor choice of industry than lack of ability.

Don't be a Square Peg trying to fit into a Round Hole. *DO YOU!*

The phrase *"do you"* is a Hip-Hop term. It suggests that one should focus on and do the things that they are gifted at, as opposed to trying to be like someone else. This is probably the best advice that anyone can get when it comes to their business.

There's an old saying, *"Find a job you love and you'll never work another day in your life."*

I often tell people, **"My business IS my pleasure"**.

My hustle is easy for me to operate and I have fun doing it! This is probably the single biggest reason why I am able to do the many things I do AND be successful at each one of them.

Running your business should be therapeutic for you. This is what makes working at a job worth the hassle. This is what makes the loss of sleep and extra expense worth it.

You love what you do cuz what you do is….. YOU!

FINDING THE RIGHT BUSINESS

Most people already work at jobs that they don't like or aren't good at. These jobs cause stress that takes a toll on ones mind, body and spirit. Don't make the same mistake when it comes to your business.

One of the most important factors that will determine the success or failure of your business is choosing a business that matches your personality. But, finding the business(es) that match your skills, abilities, and interests is easier said than done.

HumanMetrics provides Internet online testing in the field of personality, relationships, and entrepreneurship and has 30 years of experience in application and development of comprehensive tests. They define seven basic business types:

- **Business Leader-** can start an innovative business, advance and expand it.

- **Manager-** can retain the stability of a business and develop it.

- **Craftsman-** bases the business on his professional skills. As a rule, he works on a business-to-client basis.

- **Licentiate-** can manage a well running business or a licensed business.

- **FreeLancer-** bases his business on his professional knowledge and job skills. As a rule, he works on short-term business-to-business contracts.

- **Home Business Entrepreneur-** arranges his business at home. He operates on a business-to-client as well as on a business-to-business basis. In the latter he tries to arrange a long-term contract.

- **Analyst-** can develop, check and introduce new approaches and methods. Works in a partnership with other business types.

What is YOUR Commodity?

Each and every one is blessed with natural talents. The most successful people are those that are simply actualizing that which they do best, and capitalizing off of it. Think about the business that you've started or are considering.

1) Is it in line with our own natural talents and gifts?
2) Would you be better suited for a different field?

Taking a personality test can be very enlightening, wise and fun. It can tell you a lot about yourself AND job/business areas you may be best equipped for.

LIFE LESSON:

*According to the Jung Typology Test at humanmetrics.com, my Personality Type is **ENTJ** (Extraverted, Intuitive, Thinking, Judging).*

*My profile is described as **FieldMarshal Rational**. This is what was said of my type:*

Hardly more than two percent of the total population, the Fieldmarshals:

- *Are bound to lead others.*
- *Usually rise to positions of responsibility and enjoy being executives.*
- *Are tireless in their devotion to their jobs and can easily block out other areas of life for the sake of their work.*
- *Root out and reject ineffectiveness and inefficiency, and are impatient with repetition of error.*
- *Desire (and generally have the ability) to visualize where the organization is going, and they seem able to communicate that vision to others.*

*Another description of ENTJs by **Joe Butt** says:*

ENTJs have a natural tendency to marshall and direct. This may be expressed with the charm and finesse of a world leader or with the insensitivity of a cult leader. The ENTJ requires little encouragement to make a plan. ENTJs are often "larger than life" in describing their projects or proposals. This ability may be expressed as salesmanship.
ENTJs are decisive. They see what needs to be done, and frequently assign roles to their fellows.
According to the Jung Career Indicator™ the following is a list of my most suitable occupations:

Management in Business or Education
Politics
Military Education

Finance
Science / Technical
High School Education
Computer Programming

These are some of the results I received from a Personality Test that I ACTUALLY TOOK. For the most part, it was right on point. I would recommend that **everyone** take a personality test!

The results shouldn't be used as an exact *roadmap*, but more like a **compass** to point you in the right direction towards reaching your own entrepreneurial destination.

Hustler's Commandment #10: Know and Believe in Thyself.

BONUS CHAPTER

EVERYTHING YOU NEED TO KNOW BEFORE STARTING YOUR BUSINESS

EVERYTHING YOU NEED TO KNOW

Once you've found your true hustle, how do you get started? For those that are just beginning (or about to start over), this chapter is for you.

According to *The Iowa Small Business Development Center*, if you are looking to start your own hustle, here some questions you should ask and answer:

What niche will my business fill?
What services or products will I sell?
Is my idea practical, and will it fill a need?
Who is my competition?
What is my business's advantage over others?
Can I deliver a better quality service?
Can I create a demand for my business?

If you still think you've got a good business idea, answer these questions:

What skills and experience do I bring to the business?
What will be my legal structure?
How will my company's business records be maintained?
What insurance coverage will I need?
What equipment or supplies will I need?
How will I compensate myself?
What are my resources?
What financing will I need?
Where will my business be located?
What will I name my business?

Then, once you've got sufficient answers to those questions, try these:

Who are your customers?
Where are they located?
What are their needs and resources?
Is the service or product essential in their operations or activities?
Can the customer afford the service or product?
Where can you create a demand?
Can you compete effectively in price, quality and delivery?
How many competitors provide the same service or product?
What is the general economy of your service or product area?
What areas within your market are declining or growing?

Now of course you won't be able to answer these questions immediately; but having a list of questions like this is good to guide your thinking. If you are really on you're A-Game, you should be able to answer most of them. With the answers to these questions you are officially ready to get YOUR hustle on.

BONUS CHAPTER

MARRIED TO A HUSTLER

MARRIED TO A HUSTLER

Hustlers' Commandment #1, "*Your network is your net worth*"; applies to our personal lives just as much as our business. And due to the intimate nature of ones relationship to their mate or otherwise "significant other", it is this single relationship that can either make OR break an entrepreneur's spirit. If you are in a serious, committed relationship (or considering one) please take the words in this chapter very seriously.

"Marry the right person. This one decision will determine 90% of your happiness……….. or misery."
H. Jackson Brown Jr.

Your mate should be an asset to your life not a liability. This does not mean he/ she has to be directly involved in your business, but it does mean that they should in some way offer some type of support that will allow you to run your business more efficiently. This support can come in many forms, but broadly narrows down to 4.

1) financial support
2) moral support
3) direct assistance
4) indirect assistance

In short, **Financial Support** is when your mate "invests" money in your business; **Moral Support** is when your mate acts basically as a "cheerleader" for you and your business; **Direct Assistance** is when your mate provides hands-an assistance to your business; and **Indirect Assistance** is when your mate does performs other duties (like housework, or running errands) that are equally necessary, but are not related to your business.

Of course, an ideal situation would be to have a mate that supports you on all levels. But this would mean that they were probably sacrificing their own goals and dreams to help you with yours. I would say that if your mate was supportive in 2 areas (and you were equally as supportive of their goals), you would have a healthy balance.

In biological terms there are 2 types of relationships: **parasitic** and **symbiotic**. A *parasitic* relationship is one sided. In this case, one party feeds off of the other providing nothing in exchange (hence the word **parasite**). A *symbiotic* relationship is one in which both parties feed off of each other; therefore, providing equal benefit. **Symbiosis** is the true nature of any real partnership.

Whether in business or in marriage, a partnership is an agreement (usually secured with a contract) in which two or more parties agree to operate as one collective whole. Each party provides a different benefit of equal value while also receiving benefits from the other parties. Each party recognizes itself and its partners as a vital and necessary part of the whole.

In business, a failed partnership is one where at least one party doesn't receive or feels that it is not receiving enough benefit for that which it provides.

Unsatisfied parties often seek to end the existing partnership so they can "partner" with someone else; or they decide to work alone as a "sole proprietor".

Partnerships also dissolve because the parties have a different view of what their goal should or how to reach it (operate). These are called "irreconcilable differences".

If these business scenarios sound similar to marital problems then you understand my point.

Just like any successful business partnership/ merger/ negotiation, a successful marital relationship requires each party to open up their "books", show a solid history of growth, disclose financial & legal problems, make honest projections for the future and arrive at a common ground for goals and operation practices.

The bottom line is: Two heads are SUPPOSED TO BE better than one. Don't make the mistake of thinking that just because you have a person present in your life that they are automatically making your life "better". If you have a mate that feels more like dead weight you might need to make some serious changes.

"Women will never be as successful as men because they have no wives to advise them." **Dick Van Dyke**

Ask yourself; Are you better or worse off with your significant other? Do you have a **symbiotic** or **parasitic** relationship with your mate? And what are YOU doing to make the situation better?

TASKS:

1) **Make a list of the pros and cons of your relationship. The pros should outweigh the cons.**
2) **Remember: No one is perfect. Not even you!**
3) **Have a serious conversation with your mate to assess your relationship and individual goals.**
4) **Be honest with your mate, AND YOURSELF!**
5) **Don't let trivial disagreements become large problems. Keep the "big picture" in mind.**

A NOTE TO EMPLOYERS:

Dear Employer,

Please don't be threatened by this book. It was not written with the intent to have employees disrespect you. On the contrary, it was written to improve on-the-job performance and relations. My hope is that more people will see the value of hard work and appreciate the fact that they have a job (even when their dream is to be an entrepreneur).

*Likewise, I also hope that you will become a **facilitator**, not a **hater**, of your employees who hustle while they work. Encourage your workers to dream big and you will find them to actually do a better job for you AND be more pleasant while doing it.*

***Hustle While You Work** is a win-win method for both employee and employer. Morale and productivity will improve all around; and you (employer) will be appreciated and revered as the person that made it all possible.*

Yours Truly,

Hotep

ABOUT THE AUTHOR

During the day **Hotep** is an elementary school teacher; but this Morehouse College graduate is so much more. Hotep is owner and operator of **Skinnymen Productions**; an independent multimedia edutainment company based in Atlanta, GA. Since 1997, he has been a pioneer in Atlanta's entertainment/ media industries. Hotep is widely recognized for his out-the-box thinking, guerilla marketing tactics and his unique  *"common sense"* approach to teaching complex business, spiritual and intellectual concepts.

Under Skinnymen Productions, Hotep has produced/ directed **2 award-winning documentaries**, written **2 books**, published a **quarterly newspaper**, released **4 albums** and created a multi-media **art exhibit**. He independently controls production and distribution of his products, owns property and has amassed an impressive investment portfolio.

No stranger to the spotlight, Hotep has been featured in numerous magazines, newspapers including: **XXL, The Atlanta Journal Constitution** and **The Washington Post**. He's also been featured internationally on various T.V., radio, internet and cable programs.

*"People are looking for answers. They are tired of the old **Secret of Success** and **Get Rich Quick** scams. The way to become successful is not a secret and the only people that get rich quickly are those that are already rich or the lucky few. For the rest of us it's a matter of Knowing one's **Purpose**, Living with **Passion** and Exerting one's **Power** through a lot of hard work or......**Hustle**!*

Book Hotep: 404-294-7165
Email: info@skinnymen.com

121

CONTRIBUTING AUTHORS

Wesley Walters is a graduate of The Atlanta University Center and CEO of ERAJ Media. ERAJ Media is a full service turnkey production/post-production company. ERAJ Media works with small non-profit agencies to large corporate clients and institutions such as Morehouse School of Medicine, Emory University, WALMART and Essence magazine. Services range from 30-second spot, music video to independent films.
www.erajmedia.com

Wife, Mother, Actress and Entrepreneur, Yolanda Zellous is founder and CEO of Zellyo Productions Inc. Zellyo Productions helps women deal with the negative connotations associated with being plus size. Under this production house, Yolanda has an upcoming magazine, a series of non-fictional books, films and other media to serve this cause.
www.zellyoproductions.com

Brooklyn born Biz Barrett graduated from MIT. Although he is a seasoned software engineer with professional publications on Artificial Intelligence and Robotics with IEEE, Barrett uses his keen insight to identify ministry opportunities and strategies for empowerment. He is the CEO and co-founder of Fishnett Ministries and Producer of the UnityFest Concert Series.
www.fishnettsupport.com

Nicholas "Redd" Scott Sr. is the C.E.O. and Founder of Redd Marketing located in Atlanta,GA. Redd Marketing has played a major role in promoting and increasing sales for small and large businesses by means of "effective marketing". Nicholas "Redd" Scott Sr. is also the author on the upcoming Sales book entitled, "Service Equals Sales".
www.reddmarketing.com

CONTRIBUTING AUTHORS

Eugene E. Adams III received his B.A. from Morehouse College and an M.A. at CSU. He is a college counselor in the Los Angeles Area. Mr. Adams is also CEO of **Most Valuable Majors, LLC**. MVM provides merchandise and services for students to promote competency, competition, and contributions to their fields of study. **www.mostvaluablemajors.com**

JaWar, Chief Visionary Officer of Music Therapy 101, has given informative seminars around the U.S. He created the workshop to identify and share vital information in a step-by-step process necessary for success and ultimate longevity in the music business. MT 101 shows the attendee how to be a successful entrepreneur and arms the aspiring artist with the tools necessary to prosper as an independent in the music business. **www.gojawar.com**

124